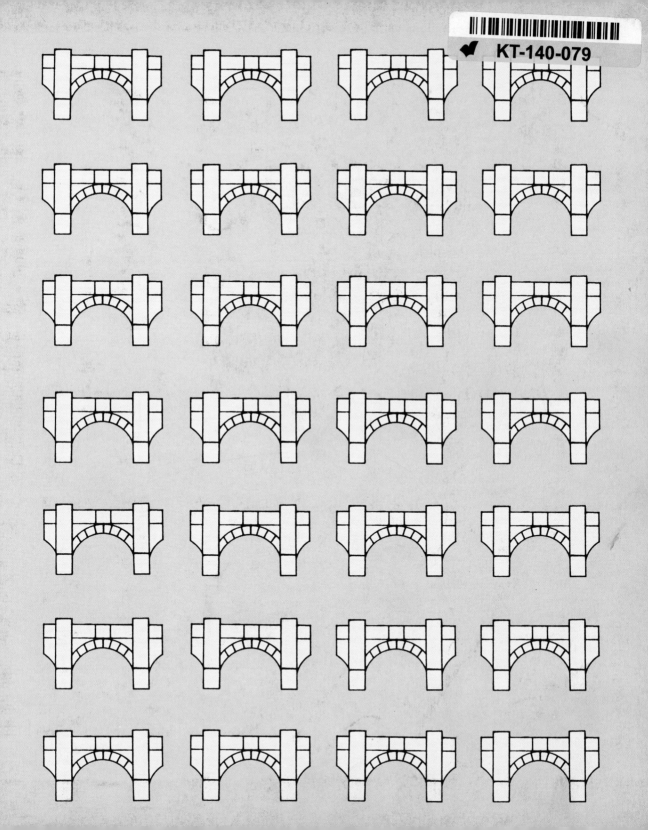

© 1994 Watts Books

Watts Books
96 Leonard Street
London
EC2A 4RH

Franklin Watts Australia
14 Mars Road
Lane Cove
NSW 2066

UK ISBN: 0 7496 1514 1

Dewey Decimal Classification Number 624

10 9 8 7 6 5 4 3 2 1

A CIP catalogue record for this book is
available from the British Library.

Editor: Sarah Ridley
Designer: Janet Watson
Picture researcher: Sarah Moule
Artists: Robert and Rhoda Burns

Photographs: Environmental Picture Library 24;
Chris Fairclough Colour Library 18, 26, 28; Robert
Harding Picture Library cover, 9, 12, 15, 21;
Picturepoint 23; ZEFA 6, 11, 16.

Printed in Malaysia

BRIDGES

Joy Richardson

WATTS BOOKS
London • New York • Sydney

Bridging the gap

Bridges make it possible to cross gaps without falling in, getting wet or going a long way round.

The first bridges were probably made from tree trunks.

Thousands of years ago, people worked out how to make stronger, longer bridges using stone.

They built up piles of stone to make columns to support the bridge. Then they laid long flat stone slabs between the columns. Some of these bridges still survive.

Arch answer

If you walk over a plank across a
wide gap, it bends in the middle.
The longer the plank, the more it bends.

Bridge-builders have to solve the problem
of how to keep a bridge up in the middle.

Early bridge-builders discovered that
the best answer was to make an arch.
They fitted wedge-shaped stones
into a curve.
As the weight on the bridge pushed down,
the stones in the arch held each other up.

Long bridges could be made with
lots of arches supporting a
straight road over the top.

Up in the air

The Romans built many arched
bridges to carry roads across rivers.
They also built aqueducts to
bring water into their cities.
The water flowed through a channel
in the stonework above the arches.

Some aqueducts had very tall arches
or several rows on top of each other.
Aqueducts were raised high over
rivers and valleys so that the water
could keep running gently downhill.

Railway viaducts still stride across valleys,
keeping the trains on a level track.

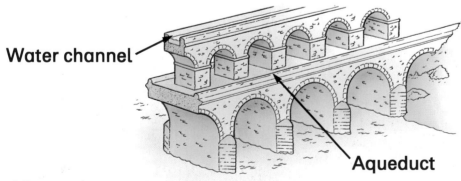

Water channel

Aqueduct

Living on a bridge

In busy towns, houses and shops were often built on top of bridges.

People, horses and carts went across the middle of the bridge between the buildings.

Narrow arches on thick columns were needed to support the weight.

Nowadays all the space on bridges is needed for traffic.

Plain bridges with no buildings can span more space with less support and leave more clear space underneath.

Iron bridge

Until about two hundred years ago,
most bridges were made of wood or stone.

Then a new bridge was built across
the River Severn in Britain.
It was the first bridge in the
world to be made of iron.

Cast iron rods were fitted
together to form an arch which
held up an iron roadway.

Iron is strong and easy to use.
Bridge-building changed for ever.

Flying arches

The simplest type of bridge
is like a plank across a ditch.
It rests all its weight on the two banks.

Many bridges are beam bridges,
supported from their two ends.
Long beams may also be held up by
arches or propped up on straight
supports, called piers.

Steel and concrete are used together
to make beams and arches which
are light but very strong.

Beam bridge

Cantilever bridge

Some bridges use cantilevers to support the beam which carries the road or railway.

A cantilever bridge has a framework of steel tubing which keeps each section perfectly balanced like a see-saw.

The Forth Railway Bridge in Scotland is a cantilever bridge.
It is a very strong structure.

Three cantilevers were positioned on supports in the river and then extended until they all met up.

FORTH RAILWAY BRIDGE

Suspension bridge

Long ago people learned to make
hanging bridges with ropes.
Today, the longest bridges in the
world are suspension bridges
which hang from steel cables.

Huge towers of steel or concrete
are set into strong foundations.
Steel cables are slung between them
and firmly anchored behind the towers.

Side cables hang down to hold
the roadway, called the deck.
The deck is hoisted up in sections
and fastened to the side cables.

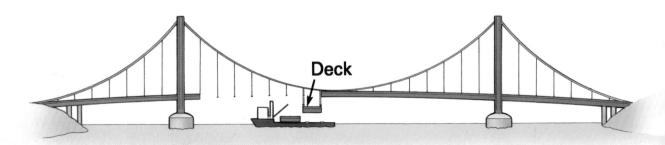

Deck

GOLDEN GATE
SUSPENSION BRIDGE
SAN FRANCISCO

Solving problems

Engineers have to solve lots of problems when they are building bridges.
They have to design a strong structure and choose building materials which will stand up to the strain.

They must work out how to keep the bridge up while it is being put together.

Foundations for the bridge supports may need to stand in water.
A special shield, called a coffer dam, has to be sunk into the ground.
Then the water can be pumped out and replaced with concrete.

Coffer dam

1   2   3   4

Over the road

Many bridges cross over roads.

Beam bridges and arch bridges
fly over motorways carrying
cars, people, farm machines or
animals to the other side.

Where motorways join,
or busy roads cross in cities,
roadways may be raised on stilts
to sweep over or under each other.

Long bridges like this are very strong.
The builders use reinforced concrete
which has steel running through it.

part of
~SPAGEETI JUNC ?

Moving bridges

Castles had wooden bridges,
which could be pulled up
on chains to keep enemies out.

Nowadays most bridges are made
to stay firmly in place but there are
still some bridges which move.

Tower Bridge in London
opens in the middle.
The two halves swing up to let
tall boats pass underneath.

Swing bridges over canals
can be turned round to let
boats through on either side.

Bridge facts

The longest bridge in the world
is the Humber Bridge in Britain.
It is a suspension bridge with nearly
1.5 kilometres between its towers.

The highest bridge is the
Arkansas River Bridge in America.
It spans a gorge almost a kilometre deep.

The widest bridge is the
Sydney Harbour Bridge in Australia.
It holds up two railway tracks,
eight car lanes, a cycle way and a footpath.

Index

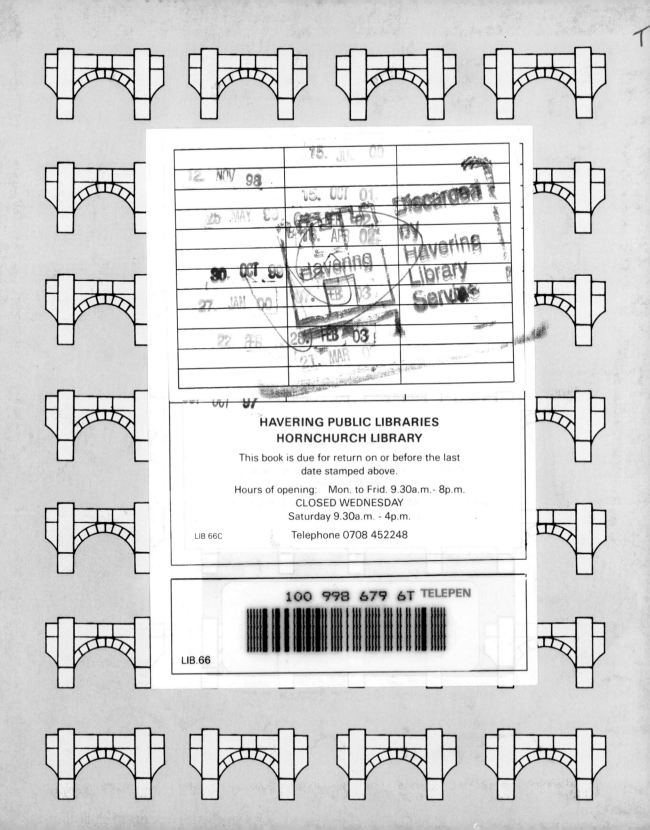